A Robbie Reader

POLAR BEARS ON THE HUDSON BAY

Dan Leathers

Mitchell Lane
PUBLISHERS

P.O. Box 196
Hockessin, Delaware 19707
Visit us on the web: www.mitchelllane.com
Comments? email us: mitchelllane@mitchelllane.com

Printing   1   2   3   4   5   6   7   8   9

A Robbie Reader/On the Verge of Extinction: Crisis in the Environment

Frogs in Danger
Polar Bears on the Hudson Bay
The Snows of Kilimanjaro
Threat to Ancient Egyptian Treasures
Threat to the Monarch Butterfly

Library of Congress Cataloging-in-Publication Data
Leathers, Dan.
    Polar bears on the Hudson Bay / by Dan Leathers.
        p. cm. — (A Robbie Reader. On the verge of extinction: Crisis in the environment)
    Includes bibliographical references and index.
    ISBN-13: 978-1-58415-586-7 (library bound)
    1. Polar bear—Juvenile literature. I. Title.
QL737.C27L398 2008
599.786—dc22
                                                                    2007000797

ABOUT THE AUTHOR: Dr. Daniel Leathers has been fascinated with the earth's environment since childhood. This fascination has developed into a career, teaching about and researching our amazing planet. He attended Lycoming College and the Pennsylvania State University, earning degrees in physics, meteorology, and geography. He currently teaches in the Geography Department at the University of Delaware. He is the author of more than 35 scientific articles and numerous popular publications. He lives in the Amish country of Pennsylvania with his wife and two daughters.

PHOTO CREDITS: Cover, pp. 4, 10, 13, 17, 20, 24, 27, 28—© 2008, JupiterImages Corporation; p. 7—Superstock; pp. 8, 19—National Geographic/Getty Images.

PUBLISHER'S NOTE: The facts on which this story is based have been thoroughly researched. While every possible effort has been made to ensure accuracy, the publisher will not assume liability for damages caused by inaccuracies in the data, and makes no warranty on the accuracy of the information contained herein.

PLB

TABLE OF CONTENTS

Words in **bold** type can be found in the glossary.

EXTINCTION

Young polar bears play in the snow. Polar bears are often born two at a time.

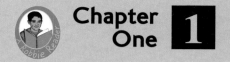
GREAT HUNTERS OF THE ARCTIC

Native peoples in the **Arctic** region of the world believe that polar bears are very special creatures. They call the polar bear *Nanuk*, and consider it to be wise, powerful, and almost like a person. Many of the native tribes tell age-old legends and myths about the polar bear. Almost all these legends have something to do with the amazing way that polar bears live in their harsh environment.

Polar bears are incredible hunters. Their favorite foods are ringed seals and bearded seals. Both types of seals live on sea ice that floats in the cold, cold waters of the Arctic Ocean or Hudson Bay. Seals are mammals, so they have to breathe air just like humans. The seals find holes in the sea ice, then they climb on top of the ice to breathe. **Leads** and **polynyas** (pah-lin-YAHS) are holes that form naturally in sea ice throughout the year. The seals also cut their own breathing holes in the ice. The native people call these holes *aglus* (AH-gloos).

Polar bears catch these seals in an **ingenious** (in-JEEN-yuss) way. They know that the seals need to come up to breathe, usually once every five to fifteen minutes. Polar bears use their powerful sense of smell to find leads, polynyas, or aglus that seals are using. Once they find a breathing hole, they wait patiently for a seal to surface. Because there are many breathing holes that seals can use, the polar bears often have to wait for many hours or even days before a seal appears.

This type of hunting may sound easy, but it's not. The bears have to travel many miles across the sea ice to find the best

A polar bear is about to feast on a seal that was captured on sea ice. The polar bear waited for the seal to come up for air, then grabbed it.

hunting grounds. The weather is extremely cold and often very windy. Also, the sea ice is constantly moving. In the winter, the sea ice moves south down to the shoreline of northern Canada, Hudson Bay, Alaska, and Russia. In the summer, the sea ice moves back to the north, and huge areas of open water are created between the shoreline and

Melting sea ice can force polar bears to swim long distances to find food. They have been known to swim over a hundred miles to find new hunting grounds. Polar bears are the only bears that depend on the sea.

the edge of the ice. In the past few decades, the amount of sea ice and its movement have been changing. These changes could cause very big problems for the polar bears.

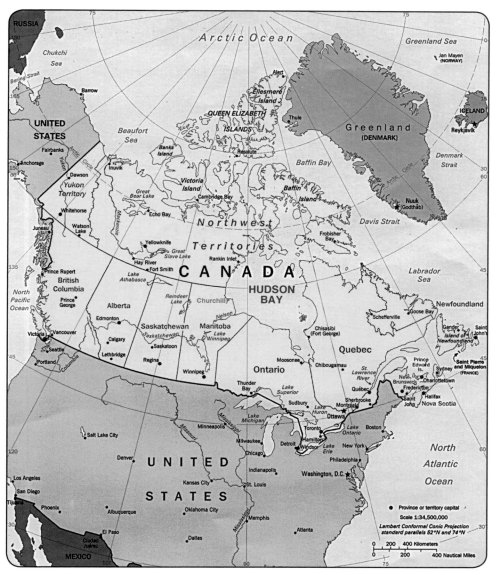

Polar bears live around the Arctic Ocean along the coasts of Alaska, Canada, Greenland, Russia, and Scandinavia (not shown). They also live along the coast of Hudson Bay. The town of Churchill, on the western side of Hudson Bay, calls itself the Polar Bear Capital of the World.

A "king of the Arctic" looks out across its harsh habitat. Polar bears have a layer of fat called blubber that keeps them from getting cold. The blubber may be over four inches thick.

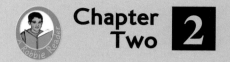

POLAR BEAR LIFE

Polar bears are found only in the Arctic region along the northern shorelines of Canada, Alaska, Russia, Greenland, and Norway. They are not considered an **endangered** (en-DAYN-jerd) species, but the number of polar bears is not large. Most scientists believe that there are between 20,000 and 25,000 polar bears living in the Arctic. Polar bears are the world's largest land **predator** (PREH-duh-tur). They are truly huge animals. Male polar bears usually weigh between 750 and 1,500 pounds, and females weigh in at 400 to 600 pounds.

Mother bears usually have two cubs when they give birth. The cubs are tiny and helpless when they are born. Most polar bear cubs are only twelve to fourteen inches long and weigh no more than one or two pounds. They depend on their mothers for everything during their first two years of life.

More than half of all polar bear cubs do not live through their first year. Some die from starvation or accidents, and some are eaten by other bears. However, if a polar bear cub makes it through its first two years, it may live a long time. Most polar bears live between fifteen and twenty years in the wild. In zoos, some polar bears have been known to live for more than forty years.

Polar bears are constantly on the move. Most walk thousands of miles each year. One bear that was tracked by scientists went on a single walk that covered more than 3,000 miles.

Polar bears don't hibernate like other types of bears. **Hibernation** (hy-bur-NAY-shun) is a long, long sleep that some bears use to make it through the winter months, when food is not easy to find. Instead of

A mother bear and her two cubs are on the move, looking for food. She will teach the cubs how to hunt.

hibernating, polar bears just continue their search for seals and any other food they can catch.

Staying clean is very important to polar bears. Clean fur keeps out the cold of the Arctic much better than dirty fur. After eating a seal or any other meal, a bear will spend a half hour or even more cleaning itself.

As the polar bears roam through the Arctic, the only creatures they have to worry about are humans and sometimes other polar bears. They have no other natural enemies.

EXTINCTION

A mother and her cubs finish a meal along the coast. The shorebirds will feast on their scraps.

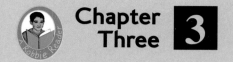
TROUBLE FOR POLAR BEARS

Even though polar bears are by far the most powerful animals living in the Arctic region, the future likely holds new dangers for them. The bears around Hudson Bay may already be feeling the effects of some of these dangers. Many human activities that take place in the Arctic are harmful to polar bears. Some of the most harmful include **pollution** (puh-LOO-shun) of the Arctic environment, oil drilling, mining, and hunting. Also, many tourists visit places like Hudson Bay each year to watch polar bears and take pictures of them. These visits can also be very hard on the bears.

It may seem strange that polar bears are being harmed by pollution. Since there are not very many people living in the Arctic, where does the pollution come from? All parts of our world are connected by the atmosphere and oceans. Pollution that is occurring in one part of the world can slowly spread across the planet.

One example of the type of pollution that is harming polar bears is a chemical called PCB. PCB is used across the world in electrical equipment, in some types of ink, and even in paper. It gets into the oceans and slowly makes its way to Hudson Bay and the rest of the Arctic. Once there, it gets into small plants and animals that are eaten by larger animals, including the seals that the polar bears eat. PCB builds up in the polar bears' bodies until it starts to harm them in many different ways.

Even polar bear cubs can be harmed by PCB. A mother bear with a lot of PCB in her body can pass this to her cubs as they are

A cub and its mother snuggle together on the snow. Cubs can become sick from pollution more easily than adult polar bears.

nursing. Since cubs are so small, even a little PCB can make them very sick.

Mining of coal, minerals, and precious stones in the Arctic has been increasing over the last 100 years. Drilling for oil and natural gas has also become much more common, especially in northern Alaska. With an increase in these activities, there is a greater chance for accidents that can harm the polar bears' environment. This can cause the bears' life to be even harder.

For thousands of years, the native peoples around Hudson Bay and across the rest of the Arctic have hunted polar bears for food and clothing and as an important part of their tribal customs. The hunting of polar bears by native peoples continues today, with over 500 bears killed each year. In most Arctic countries, the number of bears that can be killed by hunters is carefully controlled. However, many bears are killed by illegal hunting. Hunting kills more polar bears each year than anything else.

The number of tourists visiting the west coast of Hudson Bay increases every year. More and more people are also visiting other parts of the Arctic. Many of these tourists travel there because they love polar bears and want to see them in their natural **habitat**. The large number of people in the area often

Tourists and a curious bear get to know each other as the bear investigates a vehicle used for taking photos. When bears and humans come this close, it is usually bad news for the bears.

frightens the bears and makes it more likely that people and bears will come into contact. When bears and people come together, it is almost always the bears that end up hurt. Even though people don't usually mean to hurt polar bears, human activities can be very dangerous to these "kings of the Arctic."

Although it may look white, the polar bear's fur is clear, and each piece is hollow. The hair acts like the clear ice and snow of the Arctic—it reflects the sunlight, so it looks white. When the fur is oily from seal meat, it will look yellow. The skin of polar bears is black.

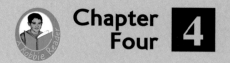

CLIMATE CHANGE

Maybe the most dangerous threat to polar bears is climate change. Over the last 100 years, the weather in the Arctic has been warming up. Over the last few decades, this warming has caused the amount of sea ice to decrease in both Hudson Bay and in the Arctic Ocean. Since polar bears spend most of their lives on sea ice hunting for seals, these changes can cause big trouble for the bears.

Around the western parts of Hudson Bay, sea ice has been forming later each autumn and breaking up earlier each spring. Because the ice is far from the shoreline for a longer time each year, polar bears have been spending more time on shore, where there is less food for them to eat. Many scientists think that this has been causing the bears to lose weight and be less healthy, especially those bears around Hudson Bay. Scientists also think that this may be causing a decrease in the number of bears being born.

Polar bears are great swimmers and will often swim as far as 50 to 100 miles to reach good hunting grounds. With the sea ice farther from shore, some polar bears are swimming up to 200 miles to reach the best hunting grounds. This is too far for many of the bears to swim, and some are drowning.

Some scientists believe that these changes have already caused the number of polar bears to decrease in some areas, especially Hudson Bay. However, in other areas the number of polar bears seems to be increasing. Some people think that the numbers in these areas are growing only because the bears are moving away from places like Hudson Bay.

A mother bear encourages her cubs to keep swimming. Their thick layer of blubber helps keep them afloat. The toes on their huge paws are webbed, which helps them swim.

Most scientists agree that if the amount of sea ice continues to decrease, problems for the bears will grow worse. Some scientists are afraid that if the climate grows warmer and warmer, polar bears may become an endangered animal or even face **extinction** (ek-STINK-shun).

For years, people have been asking governments to give polar bears more protection. In early 2007, an international group of scientists reported that global warming would continue. It would cause more melting in the Arctic, and sea levels could rise one to two feet by the year 2100. Polar bears on the Hudson Bay would lose their hunting grounds completely.

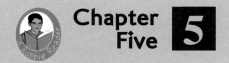
FACING THE FUTURE

Polar bears are amazing animals that have ruled the Arctic for thousands of years. An increase in the number of people in the region, and new human activities there, is beginning to cause trouble for the bears, especially the bears around Hudson Bay. In December 2006, the U.S. Fish and Wildlife Service proposed that polar bears be named an endangered species. If this happens, there may be new laws to help protect the bears from pollution, hunting, and building projects that can cause harm.

Some people believe that the warming climate in the Arctic is the biggest threat

Polar bears don't mind the cold, cold water of the Arctic and Hudson Bay. This bear is having a good time "cooling off" on a sunny day.

to the polar bear's future. Many scientists believe that the warming is caused by people polluting our atmosphere with gases that cause the earth to heat up. This theory is called global warming. Others believe that the warming is from natural causes and that human activity is not to blame.

Whatever the reason for the warmer Arctic, polar bears will have to adapt to a new environment if the climate continues to

Polar bear siblings playing with each in the summer warmth. When they are two to three years old, they will leave their family to hunt alone.

warm for a long time. The bears may have to change what they eat and where they live. Some scientists believe that polar bears will be able to change their way of life very easily, as they did when the climate changed before. Others worry that the bears will not be able to adapt quickly enough and will slowly die out until they are extinct. Whatever the answer, we humans must do our part to make sure that *Nanuk* can survive.

Polar bear survival may depend on the next move humans make.

Conserve Energy

Many scientists believe that the climate of the Arctic is warming up because of pollution in our atmosphere. The gas they believe is causing the warming is called carbon dioxide. This gas comes from burning things like oil and gas to heat our houses and power our cars. Using less oil and gas by turning the heat down in the house and walking or riding bikes instead of driving may help this problem.

Don't Pollute

You can help the bears of Hudson Bay by keeping your own environment clean. Remember that pollution in one part of the world can eventually affect another area thousands of miles away. Do everything you can to keep the place where you live free of pollution.

Learn More About Polar Bears

Read as much as you can about polar bears. There are a few books listed in the next section that will help you understand polar bears better. There are also many web sites with information about polar bears. You also may want to visit a zoo where polar bears live to see these amazing creatures for yourself.

Books

Carrick, Carol, and Paul Carrick. *The Polar Bears Are Hungry*. New York: Clarion Books, 2002.

Larsen, Thor, and Sybille Kalas. *The Polar Bear Family Book*. New York: North-South Books Inc., 1996.

Matthews, Downs, and Dan Guravich. *Polar Bear*. San Francisco: Chronicle Books, 1993.

Patent, Dorothy H., and William Munoz. *Polar Bears* (Nature Watch). Minneapolis, Minnesota: Carolrhoda Books, Inc., 2000.

Stamper, Judith, and Steve Haefele. *Polar Bear Patrol* (Magic School Bus). New York: Scholastic Inc., 2002.

Works Consulted

Stirling, Ian, and Dan Guravich. *Polar Bears*. Ann Arbor: University of Michigan Press, 1988.

Woodin, Sarah J., and Mick Marquiss. *Ecology of Arctic Environments*. Oxford, England: Blackwell Science, 1997.

Web Addresses

Defenders of Wildlife: "On Thin Ice"
http://www.defenders.org/magazinenew/Fall2001/fall01.html

National Oceanic and Atmospheric Administration—Arctic Theme
http://www.arctic.noaa.gov/essay_schliebe.html

Our Living Resources – U.S. Department of the Interior
http://biology.usgs.gov/s+t/noframe/s034.htm

Sea World Education Department
http://www.seaworld.org/infobooks/PolarBears/home.html

World Wildlife Fund – Save the Polar Bear
http://www.panda.org/about_wwf/where_we_work/europe/what_we_do/arctic/polar_bear/index.cfm

Polar Bears International—Bear Facts
http://www.polarbearsinternational.org/bear-facts/

U.S. Geological Survey: "Polar Bears in Alaska"
http://biology.usgs.gov/s+t/noframe/s034.htm

University of Alberta: "Climate Change Threatens Polar Bears"
http://www.science.ualberta.ca/nav02.cfm?nav02=21579&nav01=11471

GLOSSARY

aglus (AH-gloos)—breathing holes in the ice for seals.

Arctic (ARK-tik)—located at or near the North Pole; the word comes from the Greek word that means "bear."

endangered (en-DAYN-jerd)—threatened with danger or extinction.

extinction (ek-STINK-shun)—the dying out of a type of animal; an animal that is extinct can no longer be found anywhere on Earth.

habitat (HAH-bih-tat)—the natural environment of an animal or plant.

hibernation (hy-bur-NAY-shun)—spending the winter asleep in one small place.

ingenious (in-JEEN-yuss)—clever, inventive.

leads (leeds)—holes in sea ice.

pollution (puh-LOO-shun)—harmful chemicals in the environment.

polynya (pah-lin-YAH)—open water that is surrounded by sea ice.

predator (PREH-duh-tur)—an animal that eats or attacks other animals.